Evangelizing the Parking Lot Parent

A CATECHIST'S GUIDE TO "CASUAL-CATECHESIS" FOR FAMILIES

SR. PATRICIA M. MCCORMACK, IHM, ED.D.

TWENTY-THIRD PUBLICATIONS
twentythirdpublications.com

TWENTY-THIRD PUBLICATIONS
One Montauk Avenue, Suite 200
New London, CT 06320
(860) 437-3012 or (800) 321-0411
www.twentythirdpublications.com

Cover Illustration: ©iStockphoto.com/kchungtw

ISBN: 978-1-62785-586-0
Printed in the U.S.A.

 A division of Bayard, Inc.

CONTENTS

Introduction

What do catechists, catechetical leaders, midwives, spiritual directors, and Saint Joseph have in common? Each is an agent that accompanies another person through a season of growth. As such, each coaches a birthing process by guiding another person toward naming and claiming new life. They accompany the other through unknown territory. They mediate fears and uncertainties. They give words to the person's experiences. Often, they awaken the person to possibilities previously unanticipated. Though not responsible for creating the life that others carry within themselves, each is a catalyst for helping new life emerge.

In the case of catechists and ministers of parish faith formation programs, I am speaking of spiritual life and the process of awakening others to the person of Jesus Christ, who dwells within them and invites them into personal relationship. This is the essence of evangelization—bringing Jesus to others and bringing others to Jesus.

Where does evangelization begin? In the home! The Christian home is the privileged first place for initial evangelization. But today many parents, even churchgoing parents, voice feeling inadequate in leading their children toward intimacy with Jesus. Countless parents acknowledge a spiritual vacuum in their own lives. For a variety of reasons, some parents are unfamiliar with Church beliefs and the customs, rituals, practices, and prayer expressions that might feed the hunger of their hearts and lead them to intimacy with Jesus.

Other parents do know and practice time-honored traditions but have never transitioned from experiences of tradition to personal conviction. Catholic traditions like eucharistic devotions, Scripture prayer, varied prayer styles, Marian devotions, and the sacraments can serve as catalysts of conviction. Traditions practiced with understanding, reverence, attention, and devotion can lead to deep intimacy, encounter, and personal relationship with Jesus. Scores of adult Catholics, however, have no experience of these spiritual treasures.

Many catechists bemoan the perception that large numbers of baptized Catholic parents are disaffiliated from the Church or, at the very least, minimally, marginally, or insufficiently involved in the faith formation of their children and are themselves in need of evangelization. Reasons for this contemporary phenomenon of spiritual emptiness within adults were addressed in my previous book, *Engaging the Parking Lot Parent.* It offered a multitude of creative strategies for "backdoor evangelizing" to help parents focus on their children's faith formation while tutoring their own parent hearts in the process.

This book focuses on equipping catechists to be agents of evangelization to parents. In three significant ways, it takes parent evangelization beyond "backdoor" efforts. First, it suggests ways that catechists can meet parents where they are and function as the catalyst or midwife who brings them into an encounter with Jesus. Second, it provides experiences and material that parents can adapt to family living, thereby making home a place of spiritual richness, and faith an integral part of family life. Third, it establishes a platform for parents to be in-serviced by other parents and to build supportive networks.

Evangelization—the act of bringing the good news/the gospel—is an intentional effort to lead a person to encounter Jesus. Meeting Jesus incites a desire to know him. Knowing leads to affection. Such love spontaneously and casually overflows into passionate accompaniment, imitation, discipleship, service, and zeal to reveal Jesus in all circumstances—at home, workplace, recreational settings, prisons, shelters, and wherever two or three are gathered! "These places, which are often more loosely focused than those of the Christian community, are suitable for casual catechesis because they create more familiar relationships, and in this more visible connection with everyday life catechesis can turn out to be more compelling" (*Directory for Catechesis* 223).

Today, catechetical ministers are called to serve as agents of evangelization to parents as well as to children. Jesus is calling us to more vigorously support parents in their own faith formation. That effort implies an openness and untiring effort to be a catalyst of grace for the spiritual development of parents while facilitating faith formation programs for children. I like to think of the process as a "two-for"— "two for the price of one"; we are leading both parent and child to experiences of Jesus.

This effort challenges catechetical ministers to support, affirm, and provide resources for parents without antagonizing, offending, embarrassing, patronizing, adding stress, or implying guilt. Our goal is to energize, not to add to parent burdens or feelings of inadequacy.

St. Teresa of Calcutta said: "Very often I feel like a little pencil in God's hands. He does the writing. He does the thinking. He does the movement. I have only to be the pencil." Consider how you might become an instrument in God's hands for the benefit and encouragement of parents. Build them up. Support their efforts. Be patient with what may seem as resistance. Show the way by personal example. Let actions speak. Take things slow. Avoid overwhelming parents. Meet each parent where he/she is and respect that reality.

Engaging the Parking Lot Parent emphasized "backdoor evangelization." Rather than direct, face-to-face, adult-level sharing ("front door") the book aimed at tutoring parent hearts indirectly. It was suggested that while parents participated in activities geared to fostering faith within their children, they would encounter Jesus in the process, as a by-product so to speak. Dozens of activities provided easy-on-the-nerves, safe, face-saving, enjoyable, life-giving events.

This book focuses on direct adult evangelization. It gives catechists tools to function as effective instruments of adult evangelization in two specific ways. In part one, we look at how to engage faith-disconnected adults by providing experiences of encounter with other parents and by testifying to the ways that God has touched your life and desires to touch theirs. In part two, we look at how you can function as an agent of family evangelization by affirming parents in their role as "first heralds of the gospel"—integrating spiritual practices that complement today's family dynamics, nurturing the affective (heart) aspect of family spirituality, and celebrating the mystery and grace of the parenting vocation.

This book offers formation and information for both catechist and parent. Use the ideas as a springboard for discussion. Adapt them to suit the needs and circumstances of the families in your parish. Follow the advice of St. Teresa of Calcutta: be an instrument in God's hands.

Engage the Dis-Engaged

*"The Lord God has given me a well-trained
tongue, that I might know how to answer
the weary a word that will waken them.
Morning after morning he wakens
my ear to hear as disciples do."*

ISAIAH 50:4

Catechists, hear the call of Isaiah! It is as necessary today as it was when he proclaimed it. Adopt his perspective to "speak a word to the weary that will waken them."

There are a number of legitimate reasons many adults today are disconnected from the faith into which they were baptized and the Church from which they received Eucharist and confirmation. St. John Paul II voiced his concern about this. He said: "Entire groups of the baptized have lost a living sense of the faith, or even no longer consider themselves members of the Church, and live a life far removed from Christ and his Gospel. In this case what is needed is a 'new evangelization' or a 're-evangelization'" (*Redemptoris missio* 33). That was 1990. The number of absentee Catholics continued to increase rapidly in the years that followed.

Pope Francis speaks of accompaniment. He urges us to go to the margins, to the outskirts, to any person in need of the redeeming, freeing, revitalizing message of the gospel. Catechists need not look very far. Adults within the boundaries of your parish need to hear a word that will waken them, comfort them, and reconnect them to themselves, to their God, and to each other. Scores of adults need to meet Jesus, to encounter him, and to be encountered by him.

Catechetical leaders are uniquely positioned to provide opportunities of formation and information that help parents (and all adults) to get in touch with their own inner wisdom, to cultivate their own spirituality, to strengthen their self-confidence, and to deepen their God-relationship.

Be an Isaiah catechist! Be an evangelizing agent for parents in your catechetical community. Speak the words that touch parents in their places of need. Meet them where they are. Lead them to experiences of encounter with Jesus. Give personal testimony of how God has touched your life throughout the years, and provide exercises that will open parent eyes to how God has been present and lovingly provident in their own past histories, even though they may have been totally unaware.

The following chapters will equip you with the tools to be an Isaiah catechist.

Chapter 1

ENGAGE PARENTS IN EXPERIENCES OF ENCOUNTER

Mobility and career changes are characteristics of our times. Inherent to both is the possibility of exciting growth and surprise graces but also separation from family roots. Relocating evokes the need for new connections and expanded support systems.

In times past, a family lived close enough to grandparents, aunts, and uncles to be in frequent contact and within earshot of advice—whether it was sought or imposed. Support systems were built into the family system. Furthermore, in many neighborhoods a large majority attended the parish church and the Catholic school or the parish faith formation program. Folks crossed paths on social occasions and for school/parish events as they worked together on committees and other neighborhood projects. For most families, connection just happened.

For any number of reasons, particularly because of mobility, young parents can feel alone, lonely, and disconnected. These perceptions extend to many facets of their lives, including parenting. Folks who live close to their extended family or who live in a tight-knit community observe the parenting approaches of others and can learn vicariously which approaches are more effective than others. But those who live at a distance or in a neighborhood where families are generally private and disconnected from each other can feel as though they are parenting in a vacuum.

Here is how the parish can assist parents in encountering other parents:

- Establish a "meet and greet" program that includes visiting the home, blessing the house, and gifting the family with a faith formation "seed gift" like a prayer bowl or crucifix, or a meaningful plaque like, "Bidden or unbidden, God is present" (Carl Jung). Or, "As for me and my house, we will serve the Lord" (Joshua 24:15). Or, "Speak, Lord. Your servant is listening" (1 Samuel 3:10). Or, "Be still and know that I am God" (Psalm 46:11).

- Pair new families with veteran families to walk through "a year in the parish" together. Together, both families might attend the fall festival, the parish carol night or Christmas activity, the Advent and Lenten reconciliation services, and the parish picnic.

- Go beyond bulletin announcements and media messages about parish events. Plan instead to make a personal phone call or write a personal note—via email or snail mail—to invite the new family to join in.

- Promote a "Sunshine Club." (1) Arrange to send a "pick me up" card at specific times. (2) Host a morning coffee and/or midday snack gathering a few times during the year. Choose a timely parent topic. Provide an article to read ahead of the meeting. At the gathering discuss the article and share support. (3) Occasionally send an inspirational thought or parenting tip via text or email.

- Launch a parent book club focused on books geared to parenting support and family faith formation. Accommodate the complicated schedules of parents by eliciting sufficient volunteers to host sessions at various times.

- Set up Facebook groups and other social media sites that are more likely to invite younger parents to share ideas, information, and practices. Be intentional about setting up social media, opening up sharing and commenting permissions, and learning more about how to encourage interaction online. Post a thought, question, or article to which parents can respond and share wisdom. You might set up a group text to remind parents about upcoming events, to post a quick prayer or inspirational thought, or to refer to student assignments.

- Cultivate "vicarious learning." It is possible for parents to learn from other parents vicariously, to imagine parenting possibilities by reading the thoughts of other parents or hearing other parents share insights. Arrange a gathering—in person or online—to share the wisdom of parents. Follow the sharing with a period for silent reflection before inviting participants to share thoughts either aloud in the general assembly or within small talk groups.

Chapter 2

TESTIFY TO THE WAYS THAT GOD TOUCHES OUR LIVES

Witness, said St. John Paul II, is "the first form of evangelization" (*Redemptoris Missio*, 42). Pope Francis affirmed this: "We lead others to Jesus with our words and our lives, with our witness" (Audience to Catechists, 9/27/13). The person of the catechist, the "who" of the catechist, lends credibility to any "what" that he or she conveys. In the absence of personal witness, teachings fall on deaf ears or fail to stir the listener from thought into action.

It is not enough to tell others that God loves them, that God reaches out to them, that God welcomes them into intimate relationship, that God is faithful despite human infidelities, or that Divine Providence has been guiding them throughout their personal history. True though those sentiments are, they remain but pious sound bites in the head until a human face is put on them. You, catechist, are called to be the human face—a person just as human as the disengaged parent with whom you speak—sharing similar backgrounds, stresses, needs, desires, etc., and yet exuding vim, vigor, vitality, and enthusiasm for Jesus, for his gospel, and for your Catholic faith.

Ideally, you are an animated witness to the claim that a personal faith relationship with Jesus is possible, that it sparks life within you, and that it brings light to situations of darkness or confusion. This quality of your being attracts others. You come across as "the real deal"—a person who "walks the walk"—who continues to participate in a lifelong process of continual conversion of heart.

Witness leads to mentoring ability when you've lived through ups and downs, through spiritual feasts and soulful famines, through fidelity and sinfulness, and yet have come out on the life-giving end! In consequence, you are able to witness to a faith that is a dynamic, lively, and active process rather than a static, one-and-done condition, a faith that is more a matter of personal relationship than observance of laws and obligations, a faith that grows and deepens through ages and stages.

Disengaged parents need your personal witness. Are you able to testify to how grace has been operative throughout your life history? Are you aware of concrete occasions when you experienced God's fidelity despite your own imperfections, mistakes, and sins? Are you sensitive to the ways God's love and will have been revealed to you throughout the seasons of your life?

Here are some reflective exercises that may stir into flame your graced memories. Then, having been renewed, you might lead parents into similar exercises and share with them from personal experience.

1. LIFE HISTORY GRAPH

Prayerfully remember God's presence in your personal life history. Use paper and pencil to create a timeline that traces the ways of grace through your life. Note marker moments of highs and lows. Looking back, how did God work through those times for you? What did you learn about yourself through this exercise? What did you learn about God through this exercise? Note: It may take several prayer periods to complete this exercise. Once you "appropriate" your history of grace, you are more likely to share it in unassuming ways that give glory to God and nurture listeners' souls.

2. PERSONAL DAYENU

"Dayenu" is a song that is part of the Jewish holiday of Passover. In Hebrew the word "day" means "enough" and "enu" means "our." Therefore, *dayenu* means, "our enough"; "It would have been enough for us"; or "it would have sufficed."

This traditional upbeat Passover song has been sung for over a thousand years. It appears in the Haggadah after the telling of the story of the Exodus and just before the explanation of Passover, matzoh, and the maror (bitter herbs). "Dayenu" expresses gratitude to God for all of the gifts God gave the Hebrew nation, such as taking them out of slavery, giving them the Torah and Shabbat, and parting the Red Sea. Had God given only one of the gifts, they would have considered it "enough"—a sign of God's loving providence in their lives.

To demonstrate all the positive consequences of choosing God, the Haggadah identifies 15 specific ways that God showed his love for the Jewish people throughout history. The first five stanzas of "Dayenu" cite ways that God led them out of slavery. The second five describe miracles—i.e., how God changed nature for their benefit. And the last five tell of experiences of closeness to God. After each comment the people answer "Dayenu!" (It would have been enough)! For example: "If you had split the Sea for us and had not taken us through it on dry land, it would have been enough!"

Adapt the Dayenu concept to the blessings in your life history. Then pray your personal Dayenu. After each blessing or recognition of God's kindness to you pray: "It would have been enough." Share the Dayenu concept and your personal Dayenu with a parent group. Then provide the atmosphere for them to begin creating their own personal Dayenu.

An example, an abbreviated Dayenu recorded by one catechist follows:

- If you had exposed me to Al-Anon and had not replaced bitterness with compassion for Dad, it would have been enough.

- If you had introduced DF as a dependable teen mentor and had not given me opportunities to see myself as a capable, responsible, and self-reliant teen, it would have been enough.

- If you had provided physical and emotional safety when my marriage broke up and had not provided financial independence, it would have been enough.

3. PERSONAL PSALM OF PRAISE, PSALM 119

Psalm 119 is the longest psalm in Scripture. It is an alphabetic psalm based on the Hebrew language of 22 letters. Each verse is didactic, that is, each line is intended to teach. Each strophe of eight verses begins with the particular alphabetic letter. God's law is the focus of this psalm. The author praises God's law, statutes, commands, ordinances, decrees, precepts, words, and promises.

Adapt the alphabetic concept to form a personal psalm of praise for the gifts you have recognized during your lifetime. On lined paper, in the left margin print one letter after another vertically, from A through Z. Then, for each letter, write a subject word (or phrase) that begins with that letter and that represents a person, place, event, or experience in your life history for which you can now praise God. Pray through the memories that the exercise evokes.

Choreograph a similar experience for a parent session. Prime the pump of psalm appreciation by gifting the parents with a copy of *Reupholstered Psalms* by Greg Kennedy, SJ (Twenty-third Publications).

4. SEVEN CAPITAL GLORIES

No doubt you are familiar with the concept of the seven capital sins: pride, envy, anger, sloth, gluttony, avarice, and lust. A life-giving twist to the topic involves identifying your capital glories—your strengths, personality traits, characteristics, or skills that you have honed over time that lead you toward becoming your personal best.

Name your capital glories. Define them. Claim them as graces. What events—positive and negative—shaped you? How has God worked through your personality to shape your history? How has God worked to bring good out of situations that you once perceived to be harmful? Talk with Jesus. Then repeat this exercise in a parent session.

Caution! Every plus can become a cross. Balance is always needed. No one practices their capital glories 24x7! That said, what strengths emerge as predominant patterns through your life history? By way of example, my personal inventory includes:

- chutzpah (boldness, daring, nerve, spunk, grit, temerity);

- industry/fidelity (finish what I start, plan my work and work my plan, follow through, productivity, reliability, accomplishment);

- gadfly (a provocative goad, a stimulus that encourages, urges, drives, and moves self and others from thought into action).

5. PERSONAL MAGNIFICAT

During the Annunciation, Mary learned from the Angel Gabriel that Elizabeth was pregnant. She went immediately to support Elizabeth. During the Visitation the Holy Spirit inspired Elizabeth to recognize Immanuel within the womb of Mary. Mary validated Elizabeth and voiced her Magnificat (Luke 1:46–55)—a prayer that acknowledged God's power at work, God's fidelity to the ancient promise to send a savior, and God's salvific action within Israel throughout the ages. Mary's Magnificat was about God, not herself, though Mary was the recipient of God's love made manifest.

Reflect upon your life or a particular season in your life. Notice how God carried you or was patient with you or offered direction that changed your course for the better. Gather those incidents into a personal Magnificat.

The following example might serve as a conversation starter or a springboard for leading parents to name and claim the graces of their lives and to sense the personal affection that God holds for them—through good as well as stressful times. It was offered at the conclusion of a Magnificat retreat weekend by one of the retreatants who was going through a period of fear and confusion after losing her job.

> My soul proclaims your greatness, O my God.
> In you my spirit finds strength, healing, and
>   redirection.
> I have known your tenderness, compassion, and
>   inspiration through my ups and downs.
>
> You reached out and took me by the hand:
>
> You kept me safe and carried me when my spirit was
>   broken.
> You provided security through sufficient employment.
> You introduced me to an experienced spiritual
>   director.
> You validated my efforts repeatedly through the
>   feedback of clients....
>
> Through all events, moments, and seasons
> you remained faithful to your promises.

The appropriation statements contained in this Magnificat could also serve as Dayenu probes. Each singular statement is a grace in itself, unexpected and undeserved. Each was an experience of tender loving care, a pure gift! Precede each statement with the word "if" and respond with the mantra: "It would have been enough!" For example, *If you kept me safe and carried me when my spirit was broken, it would have been enough!*

Any of these kinds of practices testify to the ways that God has reached out and touched your soul. Such practices raise your consciousness of God's presence and God's action in your life. Consciousness moves you out of your head into your heart. It sensitizes you to recognize Jesus in the present moment, not merely in hindsight. As you become conscious of being immersed in God, boundary lines fade and the two of you unite as one. A consequence is that you easily infuse the experience of God into every encounter with other persons. Sharing your spirituality becomes spontaneous and unassuming. Others perceive that you are real and approachable, and they welcome your mentorship.

Immersion into God is a process that requires a season of growing. One experience of God via one prayer exercise is but a beginning. Pursue an active relationship with God. Open yourself to God. Regularly invite God in. Carve out time to rest in the Lord and to rest with the Lord. And when possible, create God-experience opportunities for the parent community.

When you contemplate the ways that God has reached out and touched your soul, I suggest that you begin the prayer period by praying Psalm 139. My preference is the St. Louis Jesuits' "Behind Me and Before Me," and Bernadette

Farrell's "O God, You Search Me." Then apply one of the prayer exercises presented in this chapter or devise one of your own. Conclude your prayer by expressing yourself in "I-You language" or a prayer formula that captures your spirit. Feel invited to use this prayer from my IHM Congregation:

> Loving God of my past,
> Faithful God of my present,
> Provident God of my future,
> I offer you:
> Praise, Love, Thanksgiving,
> Now and Forever.

Evangelizing the Family

"As for me and my house, we will serve the Lord."

JOSHUA 24:15

ection One addressed ways that catechists can adopt the perspective of the prophet Isaiah, who heard God's call to "speak a word to the weary that will waken them" (Isaiah 50:4). Section Two intends to help parents feel at ease in functioning as the spiritual leaders in their family. The goal is to foster the Joshua perspective within parents.

Catechetical leaders are positioned to assist parents to feel adequate, effective, creative, and comfortable in expressing their faith. Then the efforts to transmit faith to their children as well as witnessing it to others will be second nature. In short, the catechist evangelizes the parent and the parent evangelizes his/her family and community.

Be an agent of the Joshua perspective process for the parents in your parish community. Embrace the attitude of St. John Paul II, who proclaimed that "by virtue of their ministry of educating, parents are, through the witness of their lives, the first heralds of the Gospel for their children" (*Familiaris Consortio* 39). Orchestrate ways for parents to share wisdom with each other directly and vicariously via stories, suggestions, memories, and best practices. Share classroom spiritual practices that easily transfer into household practices. Spotlight family spirituality traditions, customs, and rituals that lead to a state of awareness of God's constant presence and tender love. Foster a family spirituality that nurtures habits of the heart like love for God and each other, sharing, empathy, compassion, self-control, appreciation, sensitivity, remorse, and emotional responsiveness. Be a parent cheerleader! Celebrate the vocation of Christian parenting.

The following chapters will equip parents with tools to adapt the Joshua perspective to their leadership style.

Chapter 3

AFFIRM PARENTS AS FIRST HERALDS OF THE GOSPEL

Primary Educator... First Herald of the Gospel... The hands and feet of Jesus on earth... In Loco Jesu (in the place of Jesus)... Each of these titles summarizes the vocation of Christian parenting. And each title represents merely the tip of the iceberg. What parent would not feel overwhelmed by the responsibility implied in such terms? Nevertheless, these terms identify the central role of Christian parents: to lead their child through word and example to know, love, and serve God.

There is no one way to engage parents. Nor is there assurance that every attempt will meet the need or inclination of every parent. But we can trust that the Holy Spirit will work through our good will and effort. Relax in the assurance that God began the good work of parenting and God will see to its completion (Philippians 1:6). Catechists can be the instruments, the catalysts, of encounter.

Catechetical leaders can provide opportunities of formation and information that help parent-participants get in touch with their own inner wisdom, cultivate their own spirituality, and strengthen their self-confidence. To this end I offer seven suggestions. Orchestrate each in and through non-threatening environments and exercises in which parents learn by listening to each other. View these suggestions as springboard ideas that might incite further development or adaptation.

1. In one-to-one situations informally share about your faith journey, or a time of doubt, or a marker moment from your life, etc. In other words, model how simple it may be to give faith witness. Do the same within a group gathering. State a focus (like "name a marker moment in your faith life"). Then invite parents to verbalize their response to another parent-participant. Perhaps change dyads a few times. Use opportunities with parents to encourage them to share their own faith stories with their children.

2. Host a pre-planned/pre-practiced panel discussion where parents speak to a given topic like: how they try to foster a spiritual culture in the home; how they approach teaching prayer; approaches to preparing their child for meaningful participation at Mass; how they spiritualize their home through the liturgical seasons like Advent, Christmas, Lent, Easter; or sharing examples of "God Winks"—moments when they recognized Divine Providence at work within them, or challenges they've encountered in the role of parent. Prior to another session elicit from the participants topics that they wish to experience.

3. Create a script (a dialogue scenario) or invite parents to create one that illustrates parent-child marker moments. Or, after modeling the script idea, divide parent-participants into groups of three or four and assign a topic for which they will create a script. For example, parent reviewing schoolwork with a child, correcting a child, blessing a child at wakeup, bedtime, or when leaving the house, praying before the Blessed Sacrament, sacramental preparation discussion, or issues of common interest within your community. Then engage parents and children to act out the parts for a live audience or in the form of digital media. If preferred, have students play both the role of parent and child.

IHM Sister Danielle Truex advises that creating digital media with the use of photos, video, and audio recordings can be done using a variety of platforms depending upon your technology background, available resources, and purpose. Podcasting using platforms like Adobe Spark or Canva (both have free versions) to create presentations, videos, and social media posts are ways to do this.

4. In a large space set up a Liturgical Seasons Fair. Establish sections for Advent, Christmas, Lent, Easter, Pentecost, Marian Feasts, Ordinary Time, and a section for family traditions. Engage parent volunteers to staff the sections and to provide illustrations, make-and-take crafts, ideas for home décor, cultural expressions for the season, etc. Or engage catechists from your own programs as well as catechists from nearby parishes to lead each booth.

5. *Spotlight family customs.* Around a theme like Christmas rituals or Lenten practices, invite parents and children to create a liturgical environment for their dinner table or a designated space in the home. Ask them to take photos and submit them to you with the understanding that you will create a digital presentation and post it on the parish website.

6. *Orchestrate a Words of Wisdom event that highlights multi-generational best practices.* Within a room, perhaps the church, stagger parents at various spots. One at a time spotlight a speaker who will proclaim one parent practice designed to pass on the faith to children. For example, *Whenever my children leave the house I make a sign of the cross on their forehead and I say, "I call upon the Father, the Son, and the Holy Spirit to protect you in all your ways."* Or, *Our family prays a meal blessing even when we are in a restaurant.*

Within the event incorporate guided reflection, small group sharing, and inspirational music like: "Ordinary Holiness" (Kurt & Julie Carrick, *A Couple's Rosary*); "May I Be His Love" (Kathy Troccoli, *Sounds of Heaven*); "He Who Began a Good Work in You" (Steve Green, *Find Us Faithful*); "Children Learn What They Live" (Les Crane; *Desiderata*); "Find Us Faithful" (Steve Green, *Find Us Faithful*); "My Own Backyard" (Sarah Bauer, *Radiance*), "Children Need Heroes" (Renee Bondi, *Strength for the Journey*); "An Advent Home" (Tim & Julie Smith, *Altared*—www.timandjuliesmith.com).

7. *Sponsor a Parent Fair Saturday or a Parent Retreat Day that incorporates several of these six ideas and/or additional practices.* Include a light lunch and conclude the day by celebrating the vigil Mass followed by dinner.

A major event like this requires time to develop. Share the preparation. Perhaps catechetical leaders from various parishes would each assume responsibility for one of the suggestions, offer it in his/her own parish, tweak it, and then make the program available to other parish leaders. Eventually an individual parish could combine several mini-events into a gala day. Or, designate a day to offer a **Progressive Party** where three parishes each offer a one-hour event that they repeat three times. Parents then would rotate/travel from one parish to another. Or, **Rotate Events**—Coordinate with other parishes to host one mini-event a year that draws parents from the participating parishes. Create a common calendar in order to offer these mini-events throughout the year.

Research reveals that many parents, perhaps most, second-guess themselves. Many perceive themselves inadequate to form faith (and other formation matters) within their child. They view other parents as more capable. Too many believe that faith-based education classes can fill in the gap and that catechists can do a better job in forming a child's faith than the parent can. To that conclusion I think of what my Dad would say: "Actions speak louder than words." Actions and attitudes, particularly those of a parent, speak louder than books, media, classroom activities, or the latest products of technology.

Recall for parents the power-packed promises that they made when they brought their child to baptism:

- to make it a "constant care" to train the child in the practice of the faith;

- to bring the child to keep the commandments by loving God and neighbor;

- to keep the child safe from the poison of sin;

- to help the child grow always stronger in his/her heart;

- by word and example to bring baptismal dignity unstained into the everlasting life of heaven;

- to keep the light of Christ burning brightly.

In gentle, persistent ways encourage parents to recognize and embrace the unique role they play in the spiritual formation of their children. Assure them that "God's love does not call where God's grace cannot keep." God called them to the vocation. Assure parents that God will give the graces needed to fulfill their vocation and that you, the catechist, desire to be a formative support for them.

Chapter 4

INTEGRATE SPIRITUAL PRACTICES THAT FIT WITH TODAY'S FAMILY

Parent research-participants expressed to me that they learned some parenting skills vicariously by observing how teachers work with students and through teacher-assigned home activities. With that in mind, be intentional about initiating classroom practices that can cross over and transfer into home practices.

For example, periodically invite students to teach their family the core message from a lesson, interview family members on a topic, or involve a parent's help to memorize a prayer, poem, or song that easily touches the heart. On a rotation basis, invite parents into the classroom to serve as an aide. That way, parents will be in-serviced through osmosis. You might also assign the student to replicate for the home a classroom practice (like a prayer dish, Marian shrine, post of favorite Scripture sentence), to take a photo of it, and to submit the photo to you, who will make a media presentation for all to benefit.

Most parents will not witness your classroom activities, so be creative in taking the classroom to them. For instance, a virtual tour or electronic newsletter or an electronic presentation could do the trick. If you don't have the technological expertise to do this, seek out a parent or high school student who will assume responsibility for communicating to parents the formation and information that you make available to their children in the weekly classroom setting.

Be proactive in raising parent awareness of practices that have the potential to transfer into home practices. Identify a parishioner or high schooler with computer skills who can produce family newsletters that advertise family-friendly faith practices. Or invite parents to a student-directed "open house" where the children demonstrate to their parents the classroom activities that easily overflow into home life. Make a video that showcases students involved in the classroom activities and events. Post it on the class website. Children will pester their parents to "see me!"

Here are examples of classroom practices that easily transfer into home practices.

1. Prayer Center—Reserve a windowsill, tiered corner shelving, table, or top of a filing cabinet to serve as a sacred space. It might include the liturgical color, symbols related to the feasts of the season, a thought-a-day calendar, a miniature easel to hold a focus picture or a quotation, a Bible, a rosary, child-oriented literature, a cross, a statue of Mary, a book for recording prayer petitions, etc.

2. Prayer Dish—Identify a container with a lid to serve as a common prayer vessel where students might place intentions, joys, sorrows, anxieties, etc. The contents remain private. During Advent shred the petitions and let them serve as hay for the Christmas crib. In the Spring burn them and use the ashes as fertilizer for the prayer garden. Explain that when we unite our lives with Jesus, he will repurpose them to bring new life.

3. Class Motto—Hang a banner of your class motto above the doorway, i.e., "Do whatever he tells you." "God-is-with-us-now!" Adapt Joshua's motto to read: "As for me and my class, we will serve the Lord" (Joshua 24:15). Assign families to create and hang a motto and then to send a photo that you will integrate into a slide show.

4. Lenten Practices—Brainstorm with students examples of sacrificing one good choice in order to replace it with a better good. For instance, "I will sacrifice 30 minutes of play time in order to read the Bible," or "I will give up a favorite TV show and play games with my little brother," or "I will replace 15 minutes of smartphone activity and use the time to contact my grandparents."

Additionally, engage them in creating "Fast From; Feed On" practices like, "Fast from negative remarks; feed on voicing encouragement," or "Fast from bitterness; feed on forgiveness," or "Fast from being self-centered; feed on doing for others," or "Fast from grumbling; feed on gratitude."

Share ideas aloud. Distribute recording cards (3"x5"). Direct each student to write one idea per card. Ideally, create a set of 20 cards. Minimally, create a set of seven cards, one for each day of the week. Suggest that the students put the cards in a small container and place it on the family food table so that each night a new card can be drawn for all the family to practice the following day.

5. *Conversation Starter*—Use the prayer: "May the word of God be + in our minds, + on our lips, + and in our hearts" as an introduction to serious conversation (or class, discussion, decision-making, before beginning religion homework, etc.)

6. *Annual Consecration of the Classroom*—Honor the feast of the Triumph of the Cross (September 14) by removing the crucifix from the wall and praying, "We adore you, O Christ, and we bless you because by your holy cross you have redeemed the world." Invite each student to make a physical expression of reverence and then re-enthrone the crucifix. Suggest that students lead their family to repeat this practice in every room that includes a crucifix.

7. *Hay for the Crib*—Procure an empty Christmas crib or a box to serve as a crib. Provide slips of yellow paper on which to write an Advent practice like: pray a decade of the Rosary; read a story to a younger sibling; empty the dishwasher; show kindness to three people today; visit the Blessed Sacrament; help a parent; contact a grandparent. Elicit practices from the students. Explain that the yellow slips represent hay for the Christmas crib. Motivate students to multiply their good deeds throughout Advent so as to fill the crib by Christmas. Suggest that the students replicate the activity within their own homes and engage all their family members (a) in writing practices, (b) randomly choosing yellow

slips, and (c) once completed, depositing the paper hay into the crib throughout the Advent season.

8. *Favorite Scripture Sentences*—Provide for each student a one-sided, computer-ready sheet of ten business card blocks. In eight blocks type a Scripture sentence. Assign students to cut the cards apart and to display them in a business card holder, mini-easel, or small box. Advise them to frequently change the top card and carry the thought in their heart throughout the day. Assign them to enlist the help of a parent to add two personal favorite Scripture one-liners to make a set of ten. Then, if possible, display the cards on the kitchen table or on a place in the home where it will be noticed easily.

A SAMPLING OF SCRIPTURE ONE-LINERS

"I know well the plans I have for you...plans for a future full of hope." JEREMIAH 29:11

"I have called you by name, you are mine. I will hold you always in the palm of my hand." ISAIAH 49:1, 16

"My grace is sufficient for you, for power is made perfect in weakness." 2 CORINTHIANS 12:9

"The Lord himself will fight for you; you have only to keep still." EXODUS 14:14

"Remember not the events of the past, the things of long ago consider not; see, I am doing something new!" ISAIAH 43:18–19

9. Chosen by Lot—At the beginning of each season create an event to review all the elements of the seasonal custom. Use a printer sheet of business cards to make cards for the individual use of each student or participant. Or, orchestrate the event so that one family member represents the entire family. After praying to the Holy Spirit for direction, the participant randomly (by lot) picks a card on which is written a spiritual practice that he/she will try to observe. Here are some seasonal ideas to get you started:

a. *Beatitudes:* On the feast of All Saints (November 1) the Mass gospel proclaims the Sermon on the Mount/the Beatitudes (Matthew 5:1–12). On eve of All Saints randomly choose a Beatitude card with a spiritual practice to use for the month.

1. "Blessed are the poor in spirit: the reign of God is theirs." Admit that you have needs…be open to change…realize that you are incomplete.

2. "Blessed are those who mourn: God will comfort them." Feel the hurt of others…empathize with the loss of another.

3. "Blessed are the lowly; they shall inherit the land." Allow others to be themselves…be open…adopt a quiet restraint that hears another's voice.

4. "Blessed are they who hunger and thirst for holiness; they shall have their fill." Be aware that spiritual hunger keeps priorities in a spiritual order…develop spiritual goals and motivations.

5. "Blessed are those who show mercy to others; God will show mercy to them." Develop unconditional compassion…be sensitive and free in giving yourself to others' needs.

6. "Blessed are the pure in heart, the single-hearted; they will see God." Get in touch with your inner self…be unencumbered by false images…be honest with God, others, yourself.

7. "Blessed are the peacemakers; they shall be called children of God." Bridge differences without destroying the uniqueness that God created…bring harmony to the family and community.

8. "Blessed are they who are persecuted for holiness' sake; the kingdom of heaven belongs to them." Accept hostility and hatred without fighting back… act rather than react in all circumstances.

b. *Advent Mentors:* On or before the first Sunday of Advent choose a mentor card, which focuses on a Scripture character associated with the Advent-Christmas season. Walk with that character throughout the season. What are the character's personality traits? How can that character's attitudes (positive or negative) be an influence for you? Throughout Advent use the prayer of imagination to entertain conversations like "How would you handle this?" or "How can I be like you today?" or "What ought I to avoid in my actions today?" or "What about your attitudes and behaviors should I imitate ?"

1. Zachariah (Zachary/Zacharias): Luke 1:5–24; Luke 1:67–79; Luke 1:61–66

2. Elizabeth: Luke 1:5–25; Luke 1:57–66; Luke 1:67–80

3. Mary: Luke 1:26–38; Luke 1:39–56; Luke 2:6–7, 19

4. Joseph: Matthew 1:18–24; Matthew 2:13–15; Luke 2:1–5

5. Angels: Luke 1:11–13; Luke 1:26–28, 30–31; Matthew 1:18–20; Matthew 2:12–13; Matthew 2:19–21; Luke 2:8–11, 13–14
6. Herod: Matthew 2:1–8; Matthew 2:13–15; Matthew 2:16–18
7. Wise Men: Matthew 2:1–12
8. Shepherds: Luke 2:8–18

c. *Courts of the King:* On Christmas Eve randomly select a card with a symbol and function to perform at the crib of the infant Jesus. Practice the suggestion throughout the Christmas season. Note: Some families "build" the household Christmas crèche scene together, with each member placing a figurine and praying aloud the words from their card.

1. Stable: Father, like the stable, may I be open to receive you in each way that you choose to come into my heart. Jesus, touch me with the grace of devotion to your service, and especially to your poor.
2. Crib: Father, like the crib, may I offer my heart as a place for your Son, Jesus, to dwell. Jesus, dwell in my heart and make my life filled with tender love for you and all those you send into my life.
3. Angels: Father, like the angels, may I bring the good news of your coming to all those I meet today. Jesus, give me singleness of vision and gentleness of spirit to proclaim your good news to all people.
4. Wise Men: Father, like the Wise Men from the east who studied the heavens and the Scriptures, may I watch for signs of your presence. Jesus, strengthen

my efforts to be present to you in prayer and in the Scripture.

5. Shepherds: Father, like the Shepherds who heard the song of the angels and went to seek you, may I obey your voice. Jesus, give me a listening heart, always ready to hear the prompting of the Holy Spirit and always willing to respond with love.

6. Joseph: Father, like Joseph who trusted the angel's messages that he received in his dreams, may I accept the mysteries in my life. Jesus, deepen my trust in your word, and teach me to depend on your providence in all the circumstances of my life.

7. Mary: Father, like Mary who gave a willing yes to the Angel Gabriel's announcement, may I depend totally on you. Jesus, give me the gift of faith that I may learn to rely on the power of your Holy Spirit in my life rather than on my own efforts.

8. Star: Father, like the star that revealed your love to those who sought you, may I be a light for others. Jesus, grant me the vision to recognize and to draw forth the goodness that you have placed in others.

9. Straw: Father, like the straw that became your first resting place, may I be a source of welcome to all that I meet. Jesus, let my acts of charity be the straw that strengthens and provides support for others.

10. Animals: Father, like the animals whose breath and bodies sheltered your Son during the first hours of his life as a human being, may I place my gifts of nature and grace at your disposal. Jesus, give me understanding in my relationships with others so that I may know how to respond to all who need me.

11. Bethlehem: Father, you chose Bethlehem as the place where your Son came to dwell among us. Jesus, like those who were led to Bethlehem, the *House of Bread*, lead me to a deeper love of your Real Presence in the Eucharist.

d. *New Year's Eve Resolution:* Annually choose a holy mentor (**Patron**) to walk with as a spiritual confidant; a **Virtue** to practice; and an **Intention** to remember in prayer throughout the year. On New Year's Eve randomly draw a card with that information printed on it. Examples follow. Customize the material to include patrons, virtues and intentions that reflect your parish or family needs.

PATRON	VIRTUE	INTENTION
Sacred Heart of Jesus	Extend compassion to the unloved.	Pray for families of prisoners.
Our Lady of Lourdes	Demonstrate compassion for the sick.	Pray for the chronically ill.
St. Joseph	Practice Interior Silence.	Pray for the unemployed.
Our Mother of Perpetual Help	Place confidence and hope in Mary's intercession.	Pray for those in special need.
Mother of Good Counsel	Hear the Word of God and act upon it.	Pray for pastoral counselors and therapists.
St. Anne (Mother of Mary)	Practice kindness in thought.	Pray for parents and guardians.

PATRON	VIRTUE	INTENTION
Holy Spirit	Deepen awareness of being a temple of the Holy Spirit.	Pray for candidates for Confirmation.
St. Katharine Drexel	Be generous in giving alms.	Pray for the education of the underprivileged.
St. Elizabeth Seton	Persevere in the face of difficulties.	Pray for the effectiveness of Catholic schools and programs of faith formation
St. John Paul II	Apply the gospel to daily life.	Pray for a renewed missionary spirit within the Church
St. Teresa of Calcutta	Witness to the gospel of charity.	Pray for God's most abandoned poor.
Bl. Francis Xavier Seelos	Be cheerful, even in adversity.	Pray for those suffering from cancer.
St. John Neumann	Trust in God's providence.	Pray for the well-being of immigrant people.
St. Teresa of Avila	Recognize God in ordinary circumstances.	Pray for those in contemplative life.

10. Mark the Month: Dedicate each month to a patron of the Church. Include an advertisement on your parish or faith formation website, email, or other forms of electronic transmission. Be creative in engaging students and parents to discern the patron's personality traits. Discuss ways of imitating the patron, practicing an associated virtue, celebrating his/her feast day, and memorizing a Scripture thought. Encourage families to display the monthly reminder in a prominent place.

January	St. Paul (January 25)—Faith—*"I am the light of the world"* (John 8:12).
February	St. Peter (February 22)—Hope—*"Those who cling to me, I will deliver; I will set those on high, who acknowledge my name"* (Psalm 91:14).
March	St. Joseph (March 19)—Self-abnegation and Love of the Cross—*"Any one who will come after me must practice self-denial, take up the cross, and follow me"* (Matthew 16:24).
April	Mary of the Upper Room, Counselor of the Apostles (Easter Season)—Love of God—*"You shall love the Lord your God with all your heart, with all your soul, and with all your mind, and with all your strength"* (Mark 12:30).
May	Ss. Philip and James (May 3); St. Matthias (May 14)—Love of Neighbor—*"This is my commandment, that you love one another as I have loved you"* (John 15:12).
June	St. Barnabas (June 11)—Poverty—*"Blessed are the poor in spirit, for theirs is the kingdom of heaven"* (Matthew 5:3).
July	St. Thomas (July 3), St. James the Less (July 25)—Purity of Heart—*"Blessed are the clean of heart, for they shall see God"* (Matthew 5:8).
August	St. Bartholomew (August 24)—Obedience—*"You are my friends if you do the things that I command you"* (John 15:14).
September	St. Matthew (September 21)—Meekness and Humility of Heart—*"Learn of me, because I am meek and humble of heart"* (Matthew 11:29).
October	Ss. Simon and Jude (October 28)—Mortification—*"Those that hate their life in this world keep it to life eternal"* (John 12:25).
November	St. Andrew (November 30)—Recollection and Silence—*"Jesus went up on the mountain by himself to pray"* (Matthew 14:23).
December	St. John (December 27)—Prayer—*"Mary kept all these things in her heart"* (Luke 2:51).

Consider hosting a parish event to showcase these practices. Title it, perhaps, "Family Spiritual Practices through the Year." Appoint spaces or classrooms for six presentation sites. Like a progressive party, invite the participants to rotate from room to room in ten-minute intervals. If you include a general welcome and/or conclusion, the entire event would consume no more than two hours. At each site a facilitator will give a brief overview of the topic and provide handout material to enable replication at home. If you are in a position to host a day of retreat the schedule could include hands-on family activities, a meal, and the celebration of Eucharist. Consider the following sessions:

1. *Ordinary Time* (General): Prayer Center, Prayer Dish, Family Motto, Favorite Scripture Sentences;
2. *Ordinary Time* (Fall): Annual Consecration of Home (September 14th, Feast of the Triumph of the Holy Cross), Beatitudes (November 1, Solemnity of All Saints): Mark the Months;
3. *Advent*: Hay for the Crib, Advent Mentors;
4. *Christmastime*: Courts of the King, New Year's Eve Resolution;
5. *Lent*: Lenten Practices;
6. *Easter-Pentecost*: Gifts and Fruits of the Holy Spirit.

Each of the practices in this chapter has worth independent of the others. I suspect that no family would integrate all of them into their spirituality. I submit, however, that any one practice, repeated annually, will contribute to shaping a spiritual character within the members of the family.

Chapter 5

NURTURE THE AFFECTIVE ASPECT OF FAMILY SPIRITUALITY

Spirituality is fostered more by affective than by intellectual experiences. Though recognizable elements of spirituality pass through the head they must feed the heart if they are to shape the spiritual self. Spirituality cultivates habits of the heart like love for God and each other, sharing, empathy, compassion, self-control, appreciation, sensitivity, remorse, and emotional responsiveness.

Spirituality, or spirit-mentality, is the quality, manner, or mode of responding to our experience of God in each concrete circumstance of personal life. Spirituality embraces every facet of our living and affects our relationships, duties, and choices. Parent spirituality, therefore, provides children with a spiritual heritage that is more valuable than financial inheritance.

Family spirituality, among other things, is shaped, supported, and revealed via environment, rituals, customs, and personal example. When these elements focus on God and God's loving providential care for us, they tutor the heart more than the head. They lead us into a state of awareness of God's constant presence and God's tender love for us. Comfort and security flow from knowing "who we are and whose we are," that God is both transcendent and immanent, and that God calls us into relationship.

Spirituality, transcendence, immanence, Divine Providence…pretty big words for little people, and even for many big people! Catechetical materials (books, digital sources, movies) do a terrific job of explaining these elements to children in age-appropriate ways. In quite simple terms God made each of us individually and gave us a purpose—to know God, to love God, and to serve God. God loves us with tender care and looks out for us (Divine Providence). Saints through the ages affirmed that God always wills the best for us and is able to convert bad things into good for us. For example, Saint Francis de Sales counseled: "Do not fear what may happen tomorrow; the same understanding Father who cares for you today will take care of you then and every day. He will either shield you from suffering or will give you unfailing strength to bear it." One hundred years later Blessed John Martin Moye expressed this same insight in these prayerful words: "I know that you will either preserve me from the evils I dread or turn them to my good and your glory." Blessed Moye's experience of God moved him to teach others that "God's Providence governs all things, provides for everything, arranges everything, and turns everything to good."

God is bigger than everything that God created, beyond and above it all (transcendent). And yet, at the same time God dwells within each of us (immanent). God who willed creation invites us to become friends. *The ways that we come to know, love, and serve God; to recognize God's presence within us and around us; and respond to God's invitation to friendship are called our spirituality.*

SPIRITUALITY WITHIN THE CONTEXT OF FAMILY LIFE

Would anyone dispute the irreplaceable role of family in the life of a child? St. John Paul II hailed family as "the first and fundamental school of social living" (*Familaris Consortio* 37), and more recently, Pope Francis defined family as "the privileged place for transmitting the faith" (Angelus Address, July 26, 2013). Parents are, indeed, "the first preachers of the faith" (*Lumen Gentium* 11), the "locus of catechesis" for their families (*General Directory* 255), essential and irreplaceable in the spiritual development of their children for they "influence the children in a decisive way for life" (*Catechesi Tradendae* 68).

Addressing the unique role of parents in the formation of their children, the Council fathers of Vatican II declared that "Their role is so decisive that scarcely anything can compensate for their failure in it" (*Gravissimum Educationis* 3). St. John Paul II echoed that sentiment: "Family catechesis precedes, accompanies and enriches all other forms of catechesis" (*Catechesi Tradendae* 68). He recognized the need to equip parents to fulfill the catechetical nature of their parent vocation. He encouraged individuals or institutions to employ person-to-person contacts, meetings, and all kinds of pedagogical means to help parents to perform their task.

The *General Directory for Catechesis* (225) calls parents to provide "a Christian education more witnessed to than taught, more occasional than systematic, more on-going and daily than structured into periods." What, precisely, does that entail?

"A Christian education more witnessed to than taught…"
The witness of faith-filled living more effectively evangelizes children than the words, lessons, or curriculum that parents might formally teach. Still, parents need to continue being intentional in faith formation efforts.

"A Christian education…more occasional than systematic…" When a sense of God permeates family life; when spirituality is spontaneous, informal, impromptu, and communicated with ease and familiarity (casual catechesis), it is exponentially more effective in evangelizing children than weekly, systematic lessons. Still, children need to continue formal faith formation classes.

"A Christian education…more ongoing and daily than structured into periods." When Christian formation (awareness of God, prayer, moral development, agape love, and the gospel) is *standard operating procedure* and the *modis operandi* of parents, children will more likely develop a relationship with God and overflow into service for humankind. Still, children require age-appropriate exposure to these elements in structured periods.

Authentic family catechesis leads children to know, love, and serve God. Chapters three and four presented the kinds of activities and practices that promote the values expressed by the *General Directory for Catechesis*. This chapter focuses entirely on ways that parents can permeate family life with an awareness of God.

External elements, actions, behaviors, practices, and habits can raise our awareness of God's presence and God's love for us. Here we will consider five ways for parents to nurture the affective aspect of family spirituality:

1. Prayer—*conversation* with God;
2. Environment—*physical reminders* of the sacred;
3. Rituals—*routines* that integrate awareness of God;
4. Customs—*social habits, special occasions, practices, or seasonal activities* that stir up spiritual consciousness;
5. Personal Example—*observable ways* that parents demonstrate their personal relationship with God.

PRAYER

> When parents put their newborn children to sleep, they frequently entrust them to God, asking that he watch over them. When the children are a little older, parents help them to recite some simple prayers, thinking with affection of other people, such as grandparents, relatives, the sick and suffering, and all those in need of God's help. (Pope Francis, World Communications Day, 2015)

Parents are the first to teach their children to pray in the multiple ways that Jesus prayed. He prayed formally in the synagogue. He prayed spontaneously and informally in the midst of ordinary circumstances, alone on a mountaintop, at meals, at the Last Supper, within earshot of the apostles in the garden of his agony, and from the cross. He prayed long and short prayers. He prayed aloud and in silence. In all prayer Jesus united his mind and heart with God the Father. He demonstrated that prayer is merely conversation with the One who loves us more than we can believe!

Initially **infants** experience prayer through a parent's words and blessing at bedtime and when they wake up and throughout the day; a special song or hymn performed or played electronically; or hearing the cadence of a parent praying aloud a favorite psalm like Psalm 139 as the babe snuggles on his/her chest. Prayer-ways develop as children grow older.

PRAYER-WAYS THROUGH CHILDHOOD DAYS

Pre-school-aged children (4-5) absorb simple phrases and sing-song rhyming poems and repetitive action jingles.

Kindergarten-age children (5-6) relate to simple sentences like *"Jesus, tell me what you want me to do and I will do it"* or *"Jesus loves me this I know 'cause the Bible tells me so."*

Primary school-aged children (6-7-8) can learn traditional prayers like the Our Father, Hail Mary, the Act of Contrition, and the Guardian Angel prayer.

Intermediate school-aged children (8-9-10) are able to learn additional prayers like the Rosary, the Stations of the Cross, and songs/hymns/poems that shape a Jesus-attitude, like the Saint Francis Peace Prayer.

Middle Schoolers (11-12-13) benefit from aspirations like, *"Sacred Heart of Jesus, I place my trust in you."* Or *"My Queen, my mother. Remember I am yours. Keep me, Guard me as your property and possession."* Or *"Jesus, remember me when you come into your kingdom."* Or *"Mother of Good Counsel, counsel and protect me."* Preteens can find prayer value in formulas like the Acts of Faith, Hope, and Love as well as the Divine Mercy Chaplet. Introduce them to the psalms. Often one-liners emerge that will tutor their hearts through their lifetime.

To all school-aged children, in age-appropriate ways, introduce participation at Mass as the highest form of prayer, visits to the Blessed Sacrament as an opportunity to nurture their personal spirituality by sitting in the physical presence of Jesus, and meditation as a method of centering. Many prayer aids provide meditations for children. My personal favorite is titled *In My Heart Room* (Mary T. Donse, ASC, Liguori).

Consider the other four elements that can nurture the affective aspect of family spirituality: environment, customs, rituals, and the personal example of parents. Here is a small sample of observations that came from students at St. Norbert School, Paoli, PA, and St. Jude the Apostle School, Sandy Springs, GA. I am grateful for their perceptions of how these elements show in their family lives.

1. ENVIRONMENT

Environment includes circumstances, objects, conditions, or physical surroundings. The question asked of the students was: *What things about your home environment (A) remind you of the sacred, (B) lead you to think about God, or (C) connect you to the spiritual part of yourself?*

The most frequent responses were Bible, rosary, motivational posters, blessings, prayer cards, statues, bedroom cross, framed prayers, statues of patron saints, and prayer corner. Specific responses included the following:

- We have a cross above our front door. It makes me feel closer to God.

- Next to the light in my bedroom is the cross that I got for my First Communion. Also, framed pictures from my baptism, first confession day, and first Eucharist are on my bedside table.

- In my living room we have a shelf of pictures of my family members getting baptized and receiving Holy Communion.

- There are little religious sayings taped around my house.

- I have a sentence from the Bible on my bedroom door. It gives me a good start each day.

2. CUSTOMS

Customs include social habits, special occasions, practices, or seasonal activities. The question asked of the students was: *What family social habits or practices (A) remind you of the sacred, (B) lead you to think about God, or (C) connect you to the spiritual part of yourself?*

The most frequent responses were Sunday Mass, Advent Wreath, Nativity Set, and bedtime blessing. Specific responses included the following:

- Before I go to bed my mom tells me, "Good night. And may God hold you in the palm of his hands."

- On Thanksgiving everybody writes what he or she is thankful for on a card. Then we mix up the cards and we guess who wrote the card that we picked.

- Every holy day of obligation we go to Mass, have lunch or dinner together, and then go home.

- We pray before every meal, even if we are at a restaurant. At home we use religious icons as table decoration.

- For several summers our family spent a two-week vacation at a wilderness retreat center. It included fishing, camping, hiking, arts and crafts, worship, conferences for adults, education sessions for kids, family programs, and teaching sessions about ecology, theology, and social justice issues.

3. RITUALS

Rituals include routines, established procedures, regularly practiced actions or behaviors. The question asked of the students was: *What family routines, procedures or regularly practiced behaviors (A) remind you of the sacred, (B) lead you to think about God, or (C) connect you to the spiritual part of yourself?*

The most frequent responses were praying grace before meals, goodnight prayer routines, and Sunday Mass. Specific responses included the following:

- We go to all the special Masses and go regularly on Saturdays and Sundays.

- Most nights before my mom leaves, she puts a cross on my forehead.

- We have a slogan, "Let go and let God." Also, we read a devotional every day.

- We recite a prayer before breakfast, lunch, and dinner, and if we hear an ambulance or fire truck, or if we see something upsetting on the news.

- We have a praying session at home and we watch daily Mass on the TV. We pray every morning and night and say prayers before meals. We also say the Divine Mercy prayers at 3 PM.

4. PERSONAL EXAMPLE

Personal example includes what you learn by observing another person. The questions asked of the students was: *What words or actions of your parents (A) remind you of the sacred, (B) lead you to think about God, or (C) connect you to the spiritual part of yourself?*

Specific responses included the following:

- Daily my dad attended the 6:30 AM weekday Mass. He called it "Dawn Patrol." He said that he wanted to begin each day praising God in the most effective way possible. My siblings and I were eligible to join the Dawn Patrol on our tenth birthday.

- My parents always bless me before an event like school or games. My mother always says, "You'll be okay. God is with you."

- My parents bow their heads whenever someone says the names: Mary, Jesus, God, or Holy Spirit. Every time we go to church my parents genuflect, kneel down, and pray.

- Because my parents taught me, whenever I go to Mass and the altar server rings the bell and the priest lifts up the Eucharist, I bow my head and say, "My Lord and My God."

- My family always prays before Mass begins and after receiving Holy Communion. My parents often say intentions in prayer, and I have followed that practice.

Consider replicating this mini-research project with your students. Collate the information similar to the above summary. Send the results home to parents. Or, create a prayerful period where parents assemble and hear a verbal delivery of the information. Or, use this information as a post-Communion reflection at Sunday Mass, especially at the feast of Holy Family or the Presentation of Jesus in the Temple. Parents might hear a suggestion that they never considered but will add it to their family spirituality.

Here are some additional ideas for nurturing spirituality in the home:

- Each month send home a psalm or a prayer for use at a child's bedtime. Ask the parent to pray it aloud and slowly each night for a month. Make it the last thing a child hears while falling asleep. For example, **Psalm 8** "Lord, our Lord, how majestic is your name in all the earth!…"; **Psalm 139** "You have searched me, Lord, and you know me…"; **Psalm 27** "The Lord is my light and my salvation—whom shall I fear?…"; **Psalm 23** "The Lord is my shepherd, I lack nothing….";

- At a parent meeting lead the group to experience a
  "Voice of Jesus" Prayer. Use "Hello, Jesus Speaking"
  (www.ParentTeacherSupport.org > FamilyFaith). Create
  a darkened, quiet, perhaps candlelit ambiance. Suggest
  deep breathing and relaxation. Invite them to accept
  the words that they will hear as if it is Jesus himself
  speaking. Explain that, when Jesus asks a question, you,
  the reader, will pause to give the listeners an
  opportunity to respond to the question in the privacy
  of their hearts. At the conclusion allow silence for a few
  minutes.

  Some printed sources for "God Speaking" prayers
  include:
  » A Love Letter from God the Father (www.
    FathersLoveLetter.com)
  » Jesus Initiates Conversation (www.
    ParentTeacherSupport.org > Family Faith)
  » Meditation (www.ParentTeacherSupport.org >
    Family Faith)
  » I Thirst for You. Meditation of Mother Teresa of
    Calcutta. (Ave Maria Radio/Print Document).

  Video presentations of "Voice of Jesus" prayers include:
  » www.FathersLoveLetter.com>video
  » I Thirst. www.YouTube.com. Fr. John Riccardo @
    12.06 minutes; Jake Mrugalski @ 9:07 minutes;

- As follow up, ask parents to imitate you and provide
  this kind of prayer exercise for their children. Suggest
  that parents make a tape recording of their own voice

speaking the words of Jesus and/or download the video/YouTube voices to an iPod or similar device and then gift their child with this prayer resource.

Through the expressed perceptions of children, validate the efforts of parents who are intentional about providing prayer formation, environment, customs, rituals, and example that create a sense of the sacred for their children. Encourage parents who might have been unaware of the ways that they can form faith within their children.

In *Catechesi Tradendae* (68). St. John Paul II declared, "'The church of the home' remains the one place where children and young people can receive an authentic catechesis." Here are ideas for implementing three key points in that section of John Paul's message:

Education in the faith by parents. Use the ideas in this chapter to encourage parents. Lead them to recognize and embrace the Christian vocational aspect of their parenting. Equip them to practice their vocation in such a way that no words are necessary; but that their lives alone bear witness to their children of the primacy of God and awareness of God's providential love.

Teaching the reasons behind our sacraments and sacramentals, our customs and rituals. Provide the formative support necessary for them to recognize primarily the spiritual nature of the experience and to celebrate that. Encourage families to view parties and gifts as a by-product of the social nature of the occasion, not the center of the event.

The parents as the primary educators of their children. Parish faith formation programs cannot replace the parent in responsibility or privilege. That said, parish programs are well developed, informed by Church experts, representative of the best practices in pedagogy and methods, and designed to present matters of the faith in age-appropriate ways. Encourage parents to be formed and informed by such methodical teaching. When parents and Church speak as one to children, their voice likely influences children "in a decisive way for life."

Conclusion

SUPPORT PARENTS IN THEIR VOCATION

I have long resonated with the lyrics from the song, "Getting to Know You." In the musical *The King and I* Anna sings: "It's a very ancient saying, but a true and honest thought, that if you become a teacher, by your pupils you'll be taught." This sentiment validates my experience as a teacher. It applies as well to parents who are the primary educators of their children. Saint John Paul II referred to this give-and-take dynamic. He advised parents "to follow and repeat, within the setting of family life, the more methodical teaching received elsewhere," noting that parents "profit from the effort that this demands of them, for in a catechetical dialogue of this sort each individual both receives and gives" (*Catechesis Tradendae* 68).

Faith development within any person is both taught and caught. We encourage parents to be intentional in teaching the faith within the context of family life as well as by reviewing the formal concepts that are part of the parish faith formation program. Often, in the process of child feedback, the parent becomes the student. At other times the parent is teaching unawares.

Another axiom is true: "Children learn what they live." Engage the parent community in sharing their own child- hood memories of the faith-related things that they learned through observation or through practice. Empower parents to recognize the exponential part that they play in the faith formation of their children. The source of the following re- flection is unknown but the message is spot on!

On My Heels

My three-year-old was on my heels no matter where I went. Whenever I stopped to do something and turned back around, I would trip over him. I patient- ly suggested fun activities to keep him occupied. But he simply smiled an innocent smile and said, "Oh, that's all right, Mommy. I'd rather be in here with you." Then he continued to bounce happily along behind me. After stepping on his toes for the fifth time, I began to lose patience. When I asked him why he was acting this way, he looked up at me with sweet green eyes and said, "Well, Mommy, my teach- er told me to walk in Jesus' footsteps. But I can't see him, so I am walking in yours."

A child's parents are the primary hands and feet and smile and acceptance of God on earth. Children first walk in the footsteps of their parents. When traditional practices are wo- ven into the fabric of family life they can ready the soul of a child for eventual intimacy with Jesus. The goal of Christian parenting is to be this catalyst of intimacy with Jesus. And that implies moving beyond tradition to conviction.

The practices suggested within this book do not guarantee conviction, but they increase the odds in favor of God-connections. For instance, while reflecting on ways that the home environment could foster a sense of the sacred, one student said, "Every time I look at these environmental markers I automatically feel protected by God." To that I add: These things have the potential to make us conscious of God's presence and to evoke a response within us.

Most especially, God-connection takes root when evangelization is more casual than formal; when awareness of God is more like the air we breathe rather than a lesson to master; and more a source of refreshment than a challenge or duty. To that end, adapt the suggestions within this book to benefit both your personal, on-going catechist-formation goals and the evangelization of parents whose vocation it is to permeate the family home with the presence of Jesus.

Resolve to equip Christian parents to embrace their vocation. View yourself as a midwife and companion in this divine enterprise. Strive to be:

- an agent of God's mercy, particularly during occasions of correction or misunderstanding;

- an agent of forgiveness who conveys a steady attitude of redemption, restitution, and reconciliation;

- an agent of providential care to parents and their children by anticipating need and being an ever-present source of support;

- an agent who practices "moral miracles" by delivering Jesus-like attitudes in the face of folks who challenge you;

- an agent who demonstrates that *love* and *like* are not synonyms; that love is a non-emotional choice and decision to initiate conversation, include the marginalized, heal the broken, take advantage of teachable moments, offer do-overs, use humor to defuse tension, and seek the welfare of a parent or student, even at the sacrificial price of personal convenience and preference.

By intention strive to be a catalyst of encounter to the parent community. Adapt the perspective of Isaiah to "speak a word to the weary that will waken them" (Isaiah 50:4). Meet parents where they are. Facilitate exchanges among parents. Put parents in touch with their own inner wisdom, and lead them to freedom of expression and to exercises that can deepen their God-relationship. Witness by sharing the history of your experience of God. Focus on equipping parents to be the spiritual leaders in their families. Be the agent that assists parents to feel adequate, effective, and comfortable in expressing their faith and transmitting it to others.

Well might you ask just how you can accomplish these lofty goals. My response is to place your gifts of nature and grace at the disposal of the Holy Spirit. Remember: for mere humans this is impossible, but "with God, all things are possible" (Matthew 19:26). Identify with St. Teresa of Calcutta who considered herself a pencil in God's hands. Ask God to inspire you to be an instrument of casual-catechesis for families.